ABSTRACT EXPR

A Quick Guide to Wri Abstracts for Papers a Conferences

Writing a winning abstract is an essential professional skill, but it is not a straightforward task. Good abstract writing requires a clear, cohesive and, above all, concise approach. This Quick Guide combines a set of simple strategies for abstract writing with a series of practical writing and editing exercises. Anyone who is planning on preparing an abstract for submission to a conference or who is working on an abstract for a manuscript would benefit from reading this guide.

Topics covered include:

- the structure and main components of the abstract
- practical strategies for writing an effective abstract
- the conference abstract selection process and why abstracts are not accepted
- evaluation and discussion of good/bad abstracts and strategies for improvement

Professor Allan Gaw, MD, PhD, FRCPath, FFPM, PGCert Med Ed is Director of the Clinical Research Facility at Queen's University, Belfast. He has written over 200 abstracts that have been accepted by conferences or published in journals. He is the author or editor of 17 books including the companion volumes in this series. You can learn more about him and his work at www.allangaw.com

peer reviewed
* read nutrition articles in preparation for MSc. *

Selected other works by the author

Gaw A and Burns MHJ. *On Moral Grounds – Lessons from the History of Research Ethics.* SA Press, Glasgow, 2011.

Gaw A. *Our Speaker Today – A Guide to Effective Lecturing.* SA Press, Glasgow, 2010.

Gaw A. *Trial by Fire – Lessons from the History of Clinical Trials.* SA Press, Glasgow, 2009.

Gaw A, Murphy MA, Cowan RA, O'Reilly D St J, Stewart MJ and Shepherd J. *Clinical Biochemistry An Illustrated Colour Text.* 4th edition, Elsevier, Edinburgh, 2008.

Lindsay GM and Gaw A. (Eds) *Coronary Heart Disease Prevention: A Handbook for the Health-care Team* 2nd edition, Harcourt Brace, Edinburgh, 2004.

Abstract Expressions

A Quick Guide to Writing Effective Abstracts for Papers and Conferences

Allan Gaw

SA PRESS

First published 2011
by SA Press

sapress42@gmail.com

British Library Cataloguing in Publication Data

A catalogue record for this book is available from the British Library.

ISBN 978-0-9563242-3-8

For Stephen and Alex

CONTENTS

How to use this book

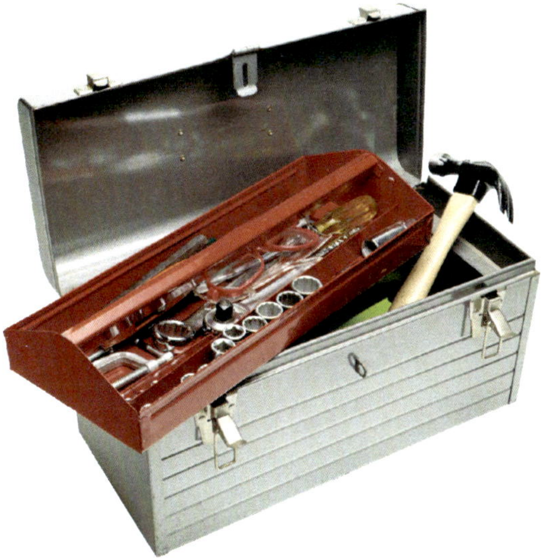

This Quick Guide is designed to be read in either a linear fashion from beginning to end, or if you prefer by dipping into the sections that interest you most.

As well as the text, which provides you with all the tools you need to write an effective abstract, I have also included a series of activities to allow you to practice your new skills. These are, of course, optional, but perhaps the only way to learn to write effective abstracts is first by reading and analyzing some and then having a go yourself. For each of the activities I have provided some comments and, if appropriate, model answers at the end of the book.

ACKNOWLEDGEMENTS

The idea for this book came out of the workshops on Abstract Writing that I have delivered in Glasgow and Edinburgh. I would therefore like to thank all the students who have attended these and who have clarified for me what the real problems of abstract writing are.

I must also acknowledge the debts I owe to those colleagues who have kindly read and commented on the drafts of this Quick Guide. These are Alex Gaw, Shona McDermott, Liz Ronald and Mike Burns. Despite their valuable input I emphasise, however, that any errors or pieces of clumsy prose that remain are entirely my own.

I must also thank other individuals and organizations for various acts of kindness that helped with researching of the topics, the sourcing of illustrations or the production of the book.

Liz Ronald – for help in taking the manuscript to the finished book.

David Tolmie – for help with the cover design.

The following photographers and artists – for kindly placing their work for use on Wikimedia Commons – Daniel Schwen (biro writing), Wolfgang Beyer (Mandelbrot Series Fractal), Dmgerman (HB pencils), Alexander Klink (pencil sharpener), Ben FrantzDale (fountain pen nib), batch 1928_44 (red fountain pen), Evan-Amos (erasers), Orange.man (keyboard), de: Benutzer:KMJ (lightbulb), Lin Kristensen from New Jersey, USA (books), Guido "random" Alvarez (highlighter pen) and Snaily (wand).

E. Ann Brown, Gillian Docherty and Ian Ford, my co-authors, for allowing me to reprint the abstract in figure 3.

The Massachusetts Medical Society – for kindly allowing me to reprint the abstract from the *New England Journal of Medicine.*

The American Association for the Advancement of Science – for kindly allowing me to reprint the abstract from *Science.*

Finally, I would like to thank the Quick Guide Series Editor at SA Press, Moira Mungall, for her generosity and patience.

INTRODUCTION

Twenty-five years ago I wrote my first abstract. I submitted it, hopefully, to the Association of Clinical Biochemists Annual Conference and, lo and behold, it was accepted. I duly prepared my poster presentation and attended the conference. While standing beside my poster (figure 1), proud but a little nervous, I noticed one of the most distinguished scientists in my field working his way along the line of posters. He paused at mine, read it, asked me a couple of questions and then as he moved on he nodded and said, "Nice work".

To say I was elated would have been an understatement. That abstract had been my ticket to the conference and that experience was the key that opened the door to an academic career that a quarter of a century later is still going strong.

The ability to write a good abstract is a key professional skill. Anyone wishing to submit a paper to either a journal or a conference will be required to produce a clear, concise and convincing summary of their work.

This summary, or abstract, will be used to judge the work and will frequently be the only component of the written work, poster display or oral presentation that is widely read.

The brevity of the writing, however, sometimes leads writers to the mistaken conclusion that little effort is required when writing an abstract. On the contrary, abstract writing arguably takes more skill, and proportionately more time, than the main text. In this Quick Guide I will look at the particular challenges posed by abstract writing and I will lay out a simple attack strategy for producing a winning abstract every time.

Fig. 1 My first abstract and first poster.

What is an abstract?

In many ways the relationship between a full paper or presentation, its abstract and its title are like fractals. A fractal is a geometrical shape, the component parts of which are smaller versions of the whole. The essence of fractal geometry is the notion of self-similarity – each progressively smaller part of the whole being similar either exactly, or more often approximately, to the whole.

An abstract is, therefore, a miniature version of the whole – a short piece of technical writing designed to summarise either a longer piece of work such as a paper, book chapter or dissertation, or to serve as a sales pitch for a presentation either in the form of a conference poster or a lecture. The abstract title may, in turn, be thought of as a miniature version of the abstract itself.

An abstract, although short, should contain all the key elements of the larger work: its background and purpose, its methods, its results and its conclusion. And, above all, an abstract should be able to stand-alone – fully understandable without reference to the larger work on which it is based.

While an abstract should contain all the information necessary to evaluate the longer work, it perhaps almost goes without saying that it should contain nothing that does not appear in the longer work.

Abstracts come in different shapes and sizes. Broadly there are two types: **informative** abstracts of original articles or conference submissions, and **descriptive** or **indicative** abstracts of review articles and some book chapters. The latter type, rather than summarising the review, indicates or describes what will be covered and only occasionally includes any specific details of methods or results.

An example of such an abstract from a review article in the journal *Science* is shown in figure 2. In this Quick Guide, I have decided not to focus on these types of abstract for two reasons – first, they are shorter, less structured and generally easier to write, and second, you usually only have to write them at a stage in your career when you have long since mastered the art of abstract writing. By the time you are invited to write a review article for the journals *Science* or *Nature* you will, by and large, have made it.

Informative abstracts, however, are where most of us start, and even here you will encounter different formats. Some, such as the conference submission abstract shown in figure 3 is a single paragraph of fairly dense text.

Alternatively, an informative abstract may be written in a structured format such as the example from the *New England Journal of Medicine* shown in figure 4, where each section is separated by a heading and a new paragraph break.

Other journals and conferences may require some hybrid between these two extremes. However, as we shall see below, the most important thing to remember about the different abstract formats is as follows: when writing any abstract you must adhere rigidly to whatever instructions are given by the respective journal editor or conference organiser – what they want is what they get.

Fig. 2 Example of an indicative abstract from a review article in the journal *Science*.

In Situ Studies of Chemistry and Structure of Materials in Reactive Environments

F Tao and M Salmeron

Abstract

Most materials and devices typically operate under specific environmental conditions, many of them highly reactive. Heterogeneous catalysts, for example, work under high pressure of reactants or in acidic solutions. The relationship between surface structure and composition of materials during operation and their chemical properties needs to be established in order to understand the mechanisms at work and to enable the design of new and better materials. Although studies of the structure, composition, chemical state, and phase transformation under working conditions are challenging, progress has been made in recent years in the development of new techniques that operate under a variety of realistic environments. With them, new chemistry and new structures of materials that are only present under reaction conditions have been uncovered.

From *Science* 14 January 2011: Vol. 331 no. 6014: 171-4 DOI: 10.1126/science.1197461. Reprinted with permission from AAAS.

Fig. 3 Example of a conference abstract.

INTERNATIONAL CONGRESS ON VASCULAR DISEASE PREVENTION
4-8 May 1998, Scottish Exhibition and Conference Centre, Glasgow

Predictors of plasma lipoprotein (a) concentration in the West of Scotland Coronary Prevention Study cohort

A. Gaw, G Docherty, EA Brown, I Ford

An elevated plasma lipoprotein (a) [Lp(a)] concentration is an independent risk factor for coronary heart disease. Plasma Lp(a) levels are believed to be predominantly controlled by the *APO(a)* gene, which encodes the apo(a) glycoprotein moiety of the Lp(a) particle. However, other parameters in the lipoprotein profile as well as co-existing disease states or personal traits have been proposed as co-variates. In order to examine these potential controlling factors in greater detail than previously possible, 1,760 unrelated Caucasian subjects were studied, from which were identified 907 with a single expressing *APO(a)* allele. This strategy was taken to obviate the difficulty in dealing with the co-expression of different apo(a) isoforms and the resulting compound plasma Lp(a) level. After cube root transformation of the plasma Lp(a) levels to normalise their distribution, a series of correlates were computed. There was no good correlation between Lp(a) concentration and any other measured lipid or lipoprotein in the lipid profile or with any other variable examined, with the important exception of the length of the expressed apo(a) isoform ($r=-0.491$, $P=0.0001$). We conclude that in this population the plasma Lp(a) concentration is not predicted by the plasma lipid profile, alcohol intake, or smoking status but is predicted, albeit incompletely, by the length polymorphism of the *APO(a)* gene.

Reprinted with permission of the authors.

Fig. 4 Example of a structured informative abstract from an original article in the *New England Journal of Medicine.*

Trial of 2009 influenza A (H1N1) monovalent MF59-adjuvanted vaccine

TW Clark, M Pareek, K Hoschler, H Dillon, KG Nicholson, N Groth and I Stephenson.

BACKGROUND: The 2009 pandemic influenza A (H1N1) virus has emerged to cause the first pandemic of the 21st century. Development of effective vaccines is a public health priority.

METHODS: We conducted a single-center study, involving 176 adults, 18 to 50 years of age, to test the monovalent influenza A/California/2009 (H1N1) surface-antigen vaccine, in both MF59-adjuvanted and nonadjuvanted forms. Subjects were randomly assigned to receive two intramuscular injections of vaccine containing 7.5 microg of hemagglutinin on day 0 in each arm or one injection on day 0 and the other on day 7, 14, or 21; or two 3.75-microg doses of MF59-adjuvanted vaccine, or 7.5 or 15 microg of nonadjuvanted vaccine, administered 21 days apart. Antibody responses were measured by means of hemagglutination-inhibition assay and a microneutralization assay on days 0, 14, 21, and 42 after injection of the first dose.

RESULTS: The most frequent local and systemic reactions were pain at the injection site and muscle aches, noted in 70% and 42% of subjects, respectively; reactions were more common with the MF59-adjuvanted vaccine than with nonadjuvanted vaccine. Three subjects reported fever, with a temperature of 38 degrees C or higher, after either dose. Antibody titers, expressed as geometric means, were higher at day 21 among subjects who had received one dose of MF59-adjuvanted vaccine than among those who had received one dose of nonadjuvanted vaccine (P<0.001 by the microneutralization assay). By day 21, hemagglutination-inhibition and microneutralization antibody titers of 1:40 or more were seen in 77 to 96% and 92 to 100% of subjects receiving MF59-adjuvanted vaccine, respectively, and in 63 to 72% and 67 to 76% of those receiving nonadjuvanted vaccine, respectively. By day 42, after two doses of vaccine, hemagglutination-inhibition and microneutralization antibody titers of 1:40 or more were seen in 92 to 100% and 100% of recipients of MF59-adjuvanted vaccine, respectively, and in 74 to 79% and 78 to 83% of recipients of nonadjuvanted vaccine, respectively.

CONCLUSIONS: Monovalent 2009 influenza A (H1N1) MF59-adjuvanted vaccine generates antibody responses likely to be associated with protection after a single dose is administered.

From *N Engl J Med* December 17, 2009 Vol: 361: 2424 – 35. DOI: 10.1056/NEJMoa0907650. Reprinted with permission from Massachusetts Medical Society.

WHY WRITE AN ABSTRACT?

As I noted in the *Introduction*, writing abstracts is an important skill for it often serves as the key to other opportunities. If you wish to be considered as a presenter at a conference, you will routinely be asked to submit an abstract of your presentation. You will be accepted or rejected solely on the basis of the abstract. If you wish to submit a manuscript for publication, the majority of journals will ask for an abstract as part of that submission. If the paper is published, the abstract will usually be the part most read and will often determine whether a reader chooses to access the full paper.

Indeed, it has been suggested that 10-500 times more people will read your abstract than will attend your presentation or read your paper (1). The abstract is therefore, arguably, the most important component of your writing.

Thus, abstracts are worthy of some detailed attention, but writing good abstracts is not necessarily straightforward. Just because they are short does not make them easy. In fact, the contrary is true.

One author has likened the abstract to poetry in comparison to the prose of the main paper (2), and it was the 17th century polymath, Blaise Pascal (figure 5), who apologised to his correspondent

The present letter is a very long one, simply because I had no leisure to make it shorter (3).

He recognised, as any abstract writer does, that concise writing is time-consuming and difficult. Economy of style is an art, but one which can be acquired through practise.

In the academic world, writing is of paramount importance for it is how we are judged. The number and quality of our publications will often determine promotion or, in more straitened times, even continued employment. This is not a new phenomenon and indeed the eminent physicist Michael Faraday, when asked by the younger William Crookes the secret of his success as a scientist, answered with the simple mantra: *Work, finish, publish.*

The ability to write an effective abstract is an essential element of this publication process - so where do you begin?

Fig. 5 Blaise Pascal (1623–1662) by Augustin Pajou. Musée du Louvre Department of Sculptures, Richelieu wing. Photograph by Jastrow.

HOW DO YOU START?

To write anything you need four things: a **deadline** – nothing is ever written without one; a **brief** – without a framework to build upon, your writing will be loose and unstructured; an **audience** – failing to consider the level of knowledge and understanding of your audience will lead to bad writing; and you need a **message** – you have to have something worth writing about.

Let me expand on each of these prerequisites in turn.

Deadlines

Little or nothing would ever be written without a deadline. Some say they love deadlines – especially the sound they make as they whoosh past. If you plan to submit an abstract to a conference there will be a very firm deadline to which you must adhere. Writing an abstract for a paper may require a deadline that is self-imposed or agreed with your co-authors or supervisors. However you arrive at it, make sure you have a deadline – without it you will find it difficult to put pen to paper.

Brief

Along with your deadline you will almost certainly have specific requirements for your abstract. Whether it is for a conference submission or a journal article there will be specifications as to the word length, the format, perhaps the overall style and usually the title and affiliations. These are not optional and failing to adhere to any or all of them will usually mean immediate dismissal of your abstract. Conference organisers, especially, are often so inundated with abstracts that they have little time to consider those that do not comply with the pre-set instructions. One of the commonest misdemeanours is that abstracts are the wrong length. Going over the word limit is unacceptable, but going significantly under is suspicious. If you do not even need, say, 250 words to sell your project, is it really that light-weight, and therefore worthy of consideration? Always use your word allocation, but never exceed it – even by a single word. That, indeed, is part of the discipline – to be able to construct your abstract within the straightjacket of their imposed rules.

Audience

Unless you know who your readers will be, and write with them in mind, your abstract will probably satisfy nobody. In general, the audience for your abstract will be your professional peers – those who work in the same field as you and understand the general background and vocabulary of the subject. However, you may be presenting at a multi-disciplinary conference or aiming to publish in a general interest journal, and in these cases you cannot make such assumptions.

Consider also that your audience, although familiar with your topic, may not have English as their first language. Such an international readership requires careful consideration when writing your abstract, as complex or idiomatic English will only serve to obscure your meaning.

At the other end of the spectrum you may be constructing an abstract for a lay audience – often grant applications or ethics committee submissions will require this. In these cases there can be no jargon and only a minimal of technical terms – all of which will require some of your precious word allocation for explanation.

Message

Your work is important and by defining your message you are aiming to communicate that importance to others. The message may be some new results from a scientific experiment, a new analysis of historical documents, or perhaps a philosophical argument. Whatever the case, your abstract will be a distillation of that larger work or larger argument. In each case the larger element should ideally exist before you attempt to write the abstract. This is not always the case.

Some choose to organise their thoughts when writing a paper by trying to write the abstract first. Some, often because of conference deadlines, submit their abstract before they have completed or occasionally before they have even started their project, in anticipation that by the time the conference comes around they will have something worth saying.

Some people choose to write abstracts simply in order to attend a meeting without having anything particular to say. Abstracts like these, with no real message, are often obvious to conference organisers and, if there is enough competition for slots at the meeting, these will be the first to hit the bin.

What rules should you follow?

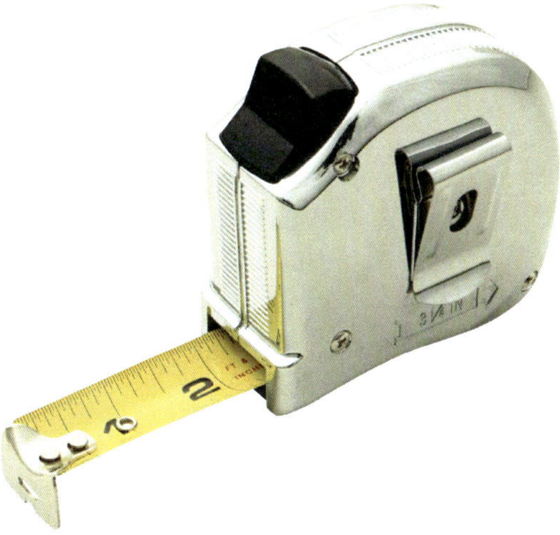

It must be noted that just as different targets require different sights – different conferences and journals will require different kinds of abstract. The most important rule to follow, therefore, in writing your abstract is to obey rigidly the set of instructions given by the editors or organisers. If they want a single paragraph of 200 words – that is what they get, and not 201 words. If they want 300 words with a series of subheadings detailing background, methods, results and conclusion – again that is what they get.

Although specific journals or conferences will require the abstract to be structured to their specifications, generally you will need to consider five components. These are the title, the background, the methods, the results and the conclusion.

Title

The title may be thought of as *the abstract* of the abstract. It is the mini-summary (usually less than 20 words) that will often be the first and sometimes the only part of the abstract that is read. It will also often be used by those skimming the conference abstract book trying to decide which sessions to attend or posters to view. It will also be used to index your published paper and must contain appropriate search terms and key words.

The title is, therefore, important and it is your opportunity to inform the reader about your work and to entice them to learn more.

As such the title needs to encapsulate three things – it must:

1. state what you did
2. state what you learned
3. capture the attention of the reader.

Many would argue that using the active voice rather than the passive voice is more effective when it comes to titles. For example, "Effects of raised cholesterol on heart attack risk" might be less arresting than "Raised cholesterol causes heart attacks".

Good titles take time to create and often emerge, like all good writing, through an iterative process of drafting and redrafting. The evolution of such a title may be charted using the following example.

Suppose you have been conducting a study looking at how magpies are referred to in literature and folklore especially when it comes to using their number to predict the future. You have used as your starting point the children's rhyme about counting magpies – "One for sorrow, two for joy, three for a girl and four for a boy…." Now you are ready to present your findings at the International Society of Ornithological Imagery, but first your abstract needs to be accepted. Your first pass at a title is:

"Magpies, myths and magic" (4 words)

This is certainly catchy with some nice alliteration, but it falls down in that it fails to tell the reader what the study was actually about and what, if anything, was learned.

The next attempt tries a little harder:

"An analysis of magpie imagery in folklore" (7 words)

Now, we have some more detail, and at least we have an idea what it was about, but we still do not know what was learned. The next attempt is a further improvement:

"Analysis of magpie imagery in English 17th century folklore: the links with prediction explained" (15 words)

Here, we now have an idea of what was done and what we can expect in terms of outcome. The abstract title has, however, in its evolution lost some of its initial punch and lacks the eye-catching quality. Can we put some of that back in?

> "One for sorrow - analysis of magpie imagery in English 17th century folklore: the links with prediction explained" (18 words)

The title now satisfies our three requirements: telling the reader what was done, what was learned and at the same time catching their eye, with the allusion to the children's rhyme at the core of the work. My only criticism of this version is that it is a little negative with the use of the word "sorrow". Other lines from the rhyme are equally eye-catching and may present a more positive image:

> "Two for joy - analysis of magpie imagery in English 17th century folklore: the links with prediction explained" (18 words)

Now, we have a potential winner.

Background

This section is required to set the scene in much the same way as the *Introduction* would in the full paper. There is usually a very great deal more that can be said by way of background about any topic than can possibly be accommodated within the confines of an abstract. While it is tempting to give a potted summary of your extensive review of the literature in this section, that is not required.

What is needed, is a simple statement of the background to the problem or issue you are addressing and what that issue or problem is. After you have read the background sentence or two at the beginning of an abstract you should be in a position to answer the following questions:

Why have these authors done this work and what is the specific problem they are tackling?

Specificity here is key, for readers want to assess quickly whether the topic of the abstract is worthy of further reading. Of course they are interested in the general topic with which you are dealing – they have picked up the journal or they are attending the conference – but what part, exactly, of this huge subject are you studying?

This section of the abstract is often the one that is criticised most by abstract reviewers. Many abstracts use as much as one third to one half of their word allocation in setting the scene. This leaves too little to do justice to the remaining sections, which many would argue are much more important – especially the results section, which may be the only original contribution in the abstract.

Methods

In this section we must set out our approach to the problem, our techniques and our methodology. Again, as in the Background section we may be tempted to try and cram in every detail of our methods, but this is neither possible, nor desirable. Your audience will have at least some knowledge of the field and the possible approaches that may be used to study it. You do not have to remind them how to perform standard techniques and tests, and you may safely make some assumptions about their skill level.

If you have used an especially novel laboratory technique, statistical method or analytical approach, then it may be appropriate to use up a little more space than usual on this, but again economy of style must prevail. After you have read the methods section you should be in a position to answer the following questions:

> *How did they do it,* as well as details such as *with what, when and with how many?*

Results

Rarely is there a problem in having too little to say here, and you will be keen to include as many results as you can pack in. Resist this urge, and concentrate on the key findings that relate to the specific research question you are attempting to answer. This may be a single finding with perhaps one or two supplementary details if there is space. The results in quantitative research should routinely be presented with appropriate statistical analyses to support their significance or otherwise. After you have read the results section you should be in a position to answer the following questions:

> *What did they find and what did they learn?*

Conclusion

The conclusion should rarely be more than a single concluding sentence with one clear idea stated. This is not the place to start expounding on what your results may mean, or what the next steps in your research project will be, or even potential deficiencies of your approach. Rather you are required to state in unequivocal, simple English what was the result, its implications, if any, and why it is worth reporting.

After you have read the final conclusion sentence of the abstract you should be in a position to answer the following questions:

> *What is important about these results* – or to put it bluntly, *so what?*

How should you write the first draft?

Writing presents many people with a problem. They simply do not know where to start, or indeed how to start. Sometimes this is simply a confidence issue that may be the result of inexperience. At other times it may be that they have no clear idea in their minds as to the story they are trying to tell. The solution to the former is practice – the more you write the easier it undoubtedly becomes. The solution to the latter is to do the necessary work before putting pen to paper. This may involve simply discussing your research with colleagues, talking it over with friends and if possible your relatives. Having to explain your work to your grandmother is a sobering experience, but a very useful one, for it will force you to work out a narrative that is both simple and understandable.

When it comes to writing the body of your abstract, there are broadly three approaches that you can take:

Option 1 - Editing a free flow

As it is easier to write a longer piece than a short one, start by writing your abstract without any word-limit in mind – just tell the whole story. Then, edit it down by removing extra sentences, extraneous words and rephrasing where possible to shorten the piece. This is one of the commonest approaches, but not necessarily the easiest.

Option 2 - Cut and paste

If you have already written the longer piece that you are now trying to summarise, pick the best sentences from the introduction, methods, results and discussion sections. Paste these together and smooth over the joins with some extra words. Unless, however, you are a skilled plasterer the joins may show and you may find this method time consuming, even though you initially thought it appealing for the opposite reason.

Option 3 - One thought – one sentence

Start as you mean to go on. Distil the background to your topic into one sentence of no more than about 25 words. Next, again in one sentence, describe your methods. In another single sentence describe your results and in a final sentence discuss their significance. Thus, you will have a bare-bones abstract of around 100 words. This will allow you to add perhaps an extra sentence in the background section, an additional sentence expanding on your methods and results and perhaps an additional sentence to explain the importance of your findings. This method does mean that most of the editing is done in your mind rather than on paper, and some find it more than difficult, in which case back to option 1.

The option you choose will depend on how your mind works. We are all different and there is no right way to write – only the way that works best for you and gets the job done.

What should you think about when writing?

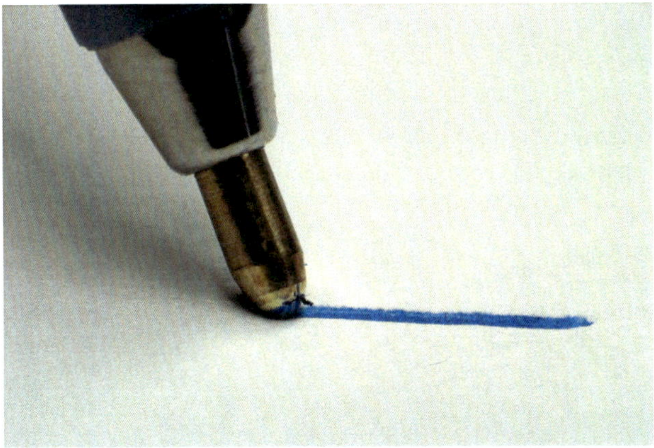

Abstract writing is a form of technical writing and as such must follow its rules and conventions, as well as the normal rules of good English. The Four Cs of abstract writing are regularly cited (4). Your abstract should be:

- **Complete** — it must cover the major parts of the project.
- **Concise** — it should contain no excess wordiness or unnecessary information.
- **Clear** — it must be readable, well organized, and not too jargon-laden.
- **Cohesive** — it should flow smoothly between the sections.

To satisfy the four Cs we must consider the words we choose, the sentences we construct, the grammar we use and our overall style. Let us look at these in turn.

The words we choose should be as simple as possible, and we should always avoid colloquialisms and jargon. Of course, we will have to include technical terms, but unnecessary or excessive use of non-standard words only serves to fog over what should be a very clear piece of writing. Although it will reduce your word count do not use contractions – like *don't*. It will lend an unprofessional air to your work and is generally not considered acceptable in technical writing.

Sentences should be short and ideally they should contain only one thought. Simple sentences are not, as some believe, an indicator of simple work. To be able to write simply is a talent much admired, but one that is difficult to acquire. Keeping your sentences short and free of unnecessary words is not only important when it comes to making your writing clear, it will also keep you within your allocated word count. Strategies for editing down a text are discussed in the next section.

The use of good grammar ensures that your abstract is readable and makes sense. Apart from the multitude of common grammatical errors that are possible to make, as part of general writing, one of the commonest grammatical problems encountered in abstract writing is the inconsistent or inappropriate use of verb tenses. Ideally, the tenses used in the abstract should be the same as those used in the paper or the presentation. Generally, the present tense is used to describe the background of the topic – this *is* the problem – and the conclusion – this result *means*…; the past tense is used to describe the methods and results – this *was* done, we *found* that…; and in addition to the present tense, the future tense may also be used in the conclusion – this *will* happen now.

Overall, consistent verb tenses should be used within sections and the entire abstract should be coherent. If you have concerns about your grammar or syntax, make sure you seek help, and remember a friend or family member may be more useful here than a colleague, as a non-technical reader may be in the best position to decide if the abstract "reads well".

If English is not your first language you should also seek the help of friends and colleagues for another reason. No matter how fluent you think you are, it is always useful to seek the help of a native speaker. An abstract is a constrained and highly technical piece of writing that may end up sounding telegraphic or disjointed even though it may be grammatically correct. Often only a native speaker will be able to tell you this. And, if they do, believe them and make some changes.

When it comes to style, there are a number of simple rules for all technical writing that we should follow.

Although in the past much technical writing was written in the passive voice, there is a growing trend in the use of the active voice. Compare: *the children were tested* with *we tested the children*, or *it is believed* vs *we believe.* In each case the former is written in the passive voice and the latter in the active voice. As the active voice often involves introducing pronouns such as *I* or *We* it is sometimes seen as creating a less formal style of writing, but it also produces a stronger, more direct style, and it is this that is now preferred by many journal editors and conference organisers.

Despite the attempts to reduce formality with the use of the active voice we are not encouraged too far along this road in modern technical writing and we should certainly avoid personal narrative and commentary, e.g. *we believe previous attempts to answer this question have produced nonsense*, or *our outstanding results will transform current thinking*.

Lastly, good technical writing is well sign-posted. By this I mean that the different sections are clearly marked and introduced. In the case of an abstract this is most easily achieved by ensuring that each section (Background, Methods, Results and Conclusion) begins with a new sentence and preferably with some indicator, e.g. *We tested this by…*, *We found…*, *In conclusion….*

How should you review and edit the text?

Abstracts are not lengthy documents and take relatively little time and effort for friends and colleagues to read. As such you should seek the advice of as many of your peers and supervisors as possible. Importantly, however, you must listen to their comments and redraft accordingly. There is an adage amongst authors that there is no such thing as good writing – only good re-writing. Review, revision and redrafting in an iterative fashion are key to the development of a good abstract.

Once you have written your abstract according to the principles of construction and style outlined above; once you have deleted the jargon and colloquialisms and the personal narrative; once you have corrected your spelling, grammar and syntax, you may still have a problem. Commonly you will still face the challenge of reducing the length of your abstract to fit the word allowance. To do this you need a set of writing strategies that may serve as paring knives. Ten components of your abstract may be tackled in this editing-down process (5-7).

1. Use abbreviations

Standard abbreviations, such as those used for units of measurement, e.g. *cm*, *kg*, *mmHg* and those that are widely accepted, e.g. *DNA* & *BBC* may be used without definition. All other non-standard abbreviations should be defined on first use, e.g. *Epidermal Growth Factor Receptor (EGFR), Main Distribution Frame (MDF), Unfinished Object (UFO).*

Do remember, however, that words such as *shouldn't*, *isn't* and *it's* are not abbreviations, but contractions, and they have no place in good technical writing.

2. Use numbers

Writing *300* rather than *three hundred* saves you a word; writing *21%* rather than *twenty one per cent* saves you three.

3. Use plurals to eliminate articles

Often you can eliminate a word by converting a singular into a plural, e.g.

The test was performed vs *Tests were performed*

or

Each mouse was given vs *Mice were given.*

Clearly this strategy should only be used if it does not corrupt the meaning of the text.

4. Use parallel constructions

If two or more expressions are included in a sentence, especially when they are being compared, it is helpful to the reader, and often economical in terms of words, to use the same format for their expression, e.g.

Patients who were treated had a median life expectancy of 4 years, compared to 1.8 years for those who did not receive treatment. [23 words]
vs
Median life expectancy was 4 years for treated patients and 1.8 years for untreated patients. [15 words]

5. Avoid adjectival clauses

A noun may be modified by an adjectival clause, which begins with a relative pronoun (who, whom, whose, that, which), or a relative adverb (when, where, why). These are commonly used in speech, but using simple adjectives rather than such adjectival clauses can save words without any loss of meaning, e.g.

the puzzle, which was solved vs *the solved puzzle*

or

the DNA when prepared vs *the prepared DNA.*

6. Avoid empty phrases

Many words and phrases with which we pepper our speech are unnecessary when it comes to written English. Some people will begin a statement with words such as *What I'm trying to say is…* or *At the end of the day….* or *It goes without saying that…* or *In order to…* None of these phrases and the many more like them has any place in good technical writing and would be an expensive luxury in an abstract.

7. Avoid nominalisations

Nominalisation means using a noun instead of a verb, often in an attempt to sound more formal. For example, we may say *she isolated the protein* or *she argued the case*, but write about *the isolation of the protein*, or *the argument of the case.* By removing nominalisations and converting the sentence structure back to using a simple verb you can often save several words, e.g.

We ensured the management of the problem. vs *We managed the problem.*

Sometimes nominalisations can be deleted altogether without any loss of meaning, e.g.

The regimen resulted in the provision of a better outcome. vs
The regimen resulted in a better outcome.

8. Avoid prepositional phrases

Prepositional phrases begin with a preposition, e.g. *of*, *at*, *for*, *from*, or *with*, and end with a noun or pronoun. They are used to modify nouns or verbs and serve to add clarity and often colour to prose. However, in the abstract they may use up precious words.

Consider: *DNA from sheep* vs *Ovine DNA*, or, *Damage of the artery* vs *Arterial damage.*

9. Avoid weak words

Weak words are those that are overused or do not add any clarity to your writing. They come in a variety of forms and can usually be eliminated without any loss to the sense of the sentence. Many weak words are used to describe quantity, e.g. *almost, very, largely, around, close to, exactly, fairly,* while others are used as padding, e.g. *actually, really, sort of.* Consider: *Actually, he really started to feel better* vs *He felt better.*

10. Avoid favourite sentences

Every abstract's first draft contains the author's favourite sentence or phrase that is included because he or she thinks it is beautiful, charming or erudite. Such a phrase often does nothing to advance the argument of the abstract and, although painful, should be excised.

In the overall editing process it is important not to cut so much that you lose sentence structure and end up with a list of sentence fragments. It is vital that the shortened version of the text is still grammatical, however tempting it may be to sacrifice grammar for economy.

WHAT ARE EDITORS OR CONFERENCE ORGANISERS LOOKING FOR?

Any abstract submitted will be assessed either by a journal editor or a conference organiser. The only common feature of this assessment, across the board, will be that it will be done very quickly. The abstract has, after all, been written to provide busy people with a simple tool to assess the work.

The editor will scan the abstract looking for key words to help decide whether the manuscript should be sent for peer review and, if so, to whom it should be sent. The conference organiser is likely to give the abstract an equally cursory review to score it in terms of interest and relevance. What are these readers looking for and what will place your abstract at the top of their pile rather than the bottom?

If you put yourself in their place it is not hard to realise that they want crystal clarity, especially of the title, key words that jump out at them and something to grab their attention.

For conference organisers, the topic of the abstract needs to fit with the conference theme and be considered of value to the meeting. For editors, the abstract must be a quick and easy-to-read indicator of the quality of the work. In both cases the abstract must be a sampler of the topic, the quality and the novelty of the work.

Do not expect to rely on your reputation, or more commonly the reputation of your institution, when your abstract is reviewed. Often the abstract will be reviewed in a blinded fashion – i.e. your name and those of your co-authors as well as your affiliations will be deleted and only the title and content of the abstract will be available to the reviewer. Thus, your abstract must stand or fall on its own merit.

Submitted abstracts are, however, frequently imperfect and one conference organiser has cited the five commonest problems with those that he receives (7).

In his opinion, they:

1. are often too short – some being less than 50 words
2. are too long
3. do no not explain what the proposed paper is about
4. spend too long defining the general topic and not enough on particular issues addressed in the project
5. are boring.

One journal editor has also added to this list by noting that, "many of the abstracts…can best be described by the use of a homely word that refers to an infestation by a certain minute organism." (1) He was writing in 1951 and perhaps could not quite bring himself to say: "lousy", but that is what he meant. He goes on to describe some abstracts as nothing more than "expanded titles" or "table[s] of contents in paragraph form". Abstracts, he argues, need to be informative and not merely teasers announcing what will be discussed, or shown or described.

The issue of 'teasers' raised here divides reviewers. Some believe the main purpose of an abstract is to attract an audience. As well as being well-written, they would argue that an abstract should contain a teaser line – usually in the conclusion – that serves to entice people to come to the presentation or view the poster. Such a teaser may be in the form: *the wider implications of this will be discussed*, or *further results will be shown.*

Other reviewers feel strongly that abstract writers should not employ this sort of stratagem. If the topic of the abstract and the results it contains are interesting enough to attract an audience or readership they will; if they are not, they do not deserve to.

One of the main concerns of such detractors is the abstract that states simply: *The results will be discussed*, rather than including any in the abstract. Often, the reason for this is not to tease, but because the results are not yet in, or that they have not been analysed in time for the submission deadline.

Abstracts that tease to this extent, without any substance, are generally placed in the rejection pile. However, the abstracts of review articles and some book chapters – often called descriptive or indicative abstracts in contrast to the informative abstracts of original articles or conference submissions – are, as we have seen above, often written in this format. Appropriately, they indicate or describe what will be covered in the paper or chapter, rather than attempt to summarise its contents.

Overall, there is only one rule for abstract submissions and that is to follow the rules – to the letter. Check the deadline for submission if it is to a conference and stick to it. Check the requested word-count and format for the abstract and stick to it. Check how they want it submitted – either electronically or on paper – and stick to it. And, remember sometimes you have to pay to submit an abstract. If that is the case, make sure you follow their instructions. Editors and conference organisers rarely have time to deal with those who do not follow the rules, and this is understandable. If you can't read and follow a simple set of instructions about how to submit an abstract what does that say about the quality of your research?

Having your abstract accepted is one thing – planning what to do next is another. Remember, once you have written and submitted your abstract to a conference and it has been accepted, your work is not over. Now you may have to prepare a conference poster or an oral presentation – I have listed some resources at the end of the book that can help you with these tasks.

You should also be thinking about the full paper that will be developed from the work you included in the conference abstract – remember Faraday's maxim: *work, finish, publish.* If your abstract was submitted as part of a full paper and it has been accepted, congratulate yourself, but remember you may have to make some changes requested by the editor and you will have to carefully review the proofs when they arrive.

In either case, whether you submitted your abstract to a conference or a journal your work is not over until the full paper is published and listed on your CV.

CONCLUSIONS

Thus, good abstracts must be very well-written although concise; they must capture the interest of the reader in a minimum of words; and they must be written in strict accordance with the requirements of their target audience.

This may seem like a tall order, but if you find yourself begin to bemoan the difficulty of abstract writing remember the words of Albert Einstein (figure 6). He said,

If you can't explain it simply, you don't understand it well enough.

The ability to present our thoughts and arguments in clear, simple and, above all, concise language is the hallmark of understanding.

Unless we can achieve this clarity, simplicity and conciseness in our writing, perhaps we really do not understand our own work. Or, perhaps, we are simply struggling with the practicalities of good writing.

This Quick Guide has, hopefully, given you new ways to think about how you tackle such a writing task - where to start, how to draft and redraft and what to think about while you are doing it. All that's left is for you to write your own abstracts. And, the best way to get anything done is to start.

Fig, 6 Albert Einstein during a lecture in Vienna in 1921. Photograph by Ferdinand Schmutzer.

REFERENCES

1. Landes KK. (1951) Scrutiny of the Abstract. *American Association of Petroleum Geologists Bulletin* 35: 1660.

2. Weissmann G. (2008) Writing science: the abstract is poetry, the paper is prose. *FASEB J*. 22:2601-4.

3. Pascal B. (1657/2009) Letter XVI in *The Provincial Letters*, BiblioBazaar.

4. UC Regents, Four Cs of abstract writing. http://undergraduateresearch.ucdavis.edu/urcConf/write.html [accessed May 5, 2011]

5. Lang, T. Concrete Advice for Writing Abstracts http://www.tomlangcommunications.com/Abstracts_files/frame.htm [accessed May 5, 2011]

6. International AIDS Society. Abstract Writing Workshop. at:http://www.iasociety.org/Web/WebContent/File/JIAS%20Abstract%20Writing%20Outline.pdf [accessed Aug 24, 2010]

7. Remenyi D. How to write an Abstract for a conference paper. www.academic-conference.org/abstract-guidelines.htm [accessed Aug 24, 2010]

Activity I – Abstract Analysis Exercise

Objective: To reinforce your understanding of the different component parts of an abstract

Task: Study the conference abstract shown in figure 3 and identify the following five components:

1. Title
2. Background
3. Methods
4. Results
5. Conclusions

Activity 2 – Abstract Scoring Exercise

Objective: To learn how a conference organiser thinks when reviewing different abstracts.

Task: Look at the three abstracts below that have been submitted to your conference on Veterinary Immunology. Abstracts of 250 words or less have been requested and each has been submitted in the hope that it will be accepted for either an oral or poster presentation. Slots for oral presentations are, however, very limited and are usually only filled by those abstract presenters whose work is considered of greatest interest and quality.

Your task is to score the three abstracts, deciding which, if any, should be accepted for the conference, and which of those may be oral or poster presentations.

Abstract 1

Characterization study performed to 11 strains from STV-8 infected horses.

Work shows results of characterization study performed to 11 strains from STV-8 infected horses, 3 from asymptomatic seropositives, 4 from animals with rapid progression to BJE. Was compared results of bio-assay study performed by classical bio-assays, with database methods, 6/32 ruling and PSSM. All the strains (3) belonging to asymptomatic seropositives were classified as T6/NSI by all the methods, while those form rapid progressors (4) were classified as TJ by 4 methods employed, and T6/Z5 by bio-assays; nevertheless, when DNA analysis was done, 3 resulted pure Z5 and only one was T6/Z5! The mutational changes should have supported the growing of the pure Z5 variants in horses of type of clinical evolution, but phenotypic transition, was not observed in vitros. These differences shown in results given by database methods, and bio-assay ones, could be explained by means of theory of stepwise processing of sequences, which precede phenotypic change of stains. Furthermore other authors (Black and Weiss) have reported DNA predictive of CXCR4 usage in serum without any detectable replication of pure Z5 variants. We valued, predicting characteristic of database methods, and its usefulness in therapeutic decision making, also, necessity to continue studying classical assays, to deepen in its clinical utility, and in understanding of STV/BJE aetiology.

(206 words)

too little - not necessary a bad thing?
- weak structure (hard to read)
- poor Grammar
no references in abstract*

Abstract 2

Antibody responses have little effect on controlling viraemia during Retro Telovirus infection of Norwegian Blue Parrots

Background: Retro Teleovirus (RTV)-infected Norwegian Forest Dwelling Birds (FDBs) do not progress to Brachio-jejunal Eratitis (BJE) despite active viral replication. It has been suggested that higher viral loads (VLs) in natural RTV infections are due to lower anti-RTV antibody titres in RTV-infected Norwegian FDBs, which implies a protective role for antibodies in controlling VLs. We studied the impact of antibody responses on RTV replication in Norwegian Blue Parrots (NBPs).

Methods: Eight NBPs were injected sub-cutaneously with 100 μg RTV. Four NBPs received 25 mg/kg Paxiban (anti-NB30 antibody) every 5 days, from day 5 post-infection, and four NBPs served as controls receiving sham injections. VLs in plasma and tissues were determined by real-time PCR and in-situ hybridization. The major lymphocyte subsets were assessed in venous blood, lymph nodes (LNs) and intestine by flow-cytometry.

Main outcome measures:

Results: All Paxiban-treated NBPs successfully depleted NB30 cells in venous blood, LNs and intestine, as illustrated by the dynamic assessment of NB30 and NB69 cells. There was no significant difference in VLs between NB30-depleted NBPs and control birds: during acute infection peak VLs ranged from 10^6-10^7 copies/ml; during chronic infection, values ranged from 10^3-10^4 RTV RNA copies/ml. Levels of acute CD4 T-cell depletion in the intestine were similar in treated and control birds. Paxiban-induced NB30 depletion resulted in structural disruption of the germinal centers in the LNs and intestinal Peyer's patches.

Conclusions: We have shown that antibody responses play no significant role in the control of RTV viral replication during acute and chronic RTV infection in Norwegian FDBs.

(250 words)

Word count does not permit but maybe add a bit about what statistical test used, alpha level

Abstract 3

Multi-drug resistant psittacosis infection control assessment in veterinary practices in rural Madagascar

Background: New reports of inter-species transmission of multi-drug-resistant psittacosis (MDRP) in rural Madagascar force attention to improving airborne infection control (AIC). AIC information, motivation and practices among veterinary staff in such settings are poorly understood, yet critically important to inform preventive measures.
Methods: A baseline assessment to identify staff AIC deficiencies by structured interviews, closed questionnaires, and practice observations performed during July-December 2010 in rural Madagascar veterinary practices. Data were categorised into Logistic, Environmental, and Personal Behavioral domains and analyzed using the Data-Motivation-Practice (DMP) behaviour change model.
Results: Logistic deficits included: lack of standard AIC policy, poor screening of potential psittacosis cases, and inadequate isolation of psittacosis cases. Environmental deficit was inconsistent natural ventilation during winter months (compliance 35-100%). Personal Behavioral deficits included: poor face-mask use (compliance 0-89%), staff unaware of own psittacosis status (41%) and failure to seek personal psittacosis diagnosis if symptomatic (13%).
DMP model analysis of barriers indicated: high data levels; low motivation to follow local policies (59% claim as barrier to practice) and distrust in occupational health service confidentiality (18.0%); practice skill deficits included inability to deliver effective AIC instructions to new staff (53%), and poor staff face-mask skills (16% unable to wear effectively, 21% unable to check seal effectively). **Conclusions:** Assessment of veterinary staff AIC Data, Motivation, and Practice skills provide useful baseline data regarding AIC deficits and barriers to preventive strategies. Staff Data levels are high, but Motivation and Practice skills need improvement to reduce risk of inter-species MDRP transmission.

(246 words)

Too long?

ACTIVITY 3 – ABSTRACT EDITING EXERCISE

Objective: To put your new editing skills into practice.

Task: Below you will find a memo from Prof. Granger-Weasley to her two colleagues containing the first draft of an abstract she wishes to submit to an International Conference. Unfortunately, the abstract is longer than the 200 words or less prescribed by the conference organisers, has no title and is rather poorly constructed.

Using the tips outlined in this Quick Guide, redraft the abstract to increase its chances of being accepted. For comparison you will find my version in the answers appendix at the end of the book.

From the wand of Prof. Granger-Weasley

Memo: From Hermione to Ginny and Harry

The deadline for abstract submission for the International Society of Academic Wizardry is coming up in two days and I would like to submit that work we did at the beginning of the year. I have drafted the abstract but – of course – it's too long. Can you two take a wand to it and get it to 200 words or less? And we need a title. Hope you can help – I'm really keen to get to the conference – it's in Bulgaria this year and being hosted by Prof. Viktor Krumm – remember him? – I do…

Homeless Hogwarts: A Study into the reasons of

Title: ????

Authors: Granger-Weasley, H.J., Potter, H.J. & Potter, G.M.

Unemployment is a scourge. Failure of our young witches and wizards to find gainful, magical employment outside the muggle world is a serious cause for concern. Indeed, in the last ten years (between 2000 and 2010) unemployment has increased from one in ten to more than one in three (i.e. to 35%)! What could the cause of this terrible trend be? One suggestion put forward recently by the Assistant Minister for Muggle Affairs, Lady Endellion Cameron, is intriguing. She has suggested that the trend for wizarding parents to send their young to muggle schools rather than to traditional seats of magical learning, such as Hogwarts School of Witchcraft and Wizardry, in the hope of integrating them more successfully into an increasingly cosmopolitan society, may be the reason. However, no hard evidence has been gathered, thus far, to support this proposal.

In this study we've set out to test this proposal by comparing the employment of those young witches and wizards who graduate after a muggle-oriented education with those who have enjoyed a traditional magical education. In order to do this we first identified two schools – one was, naturally, Hogwarts and the other was Muggleside Secondary Modern. Using a divination charm we identified those magical graduates of Muggleside and by examining the school roll at Hogwarts we identified the corresponding list of

no place for informal words. use we have

graduates there over the five year period between 2001 and 2006. All in all, we identified 256 graduates of Hogwarts School and 287 graduates of Muggleside High. All 543 were sent a parchment questionnaire using standard owl post. The questionnaire was set up in such a way as to obtain simple answers using a closed question design. 253 Hogwarts alumni responded compared with 250 of those graduating from Muggleside Secondary Modern.

When we compared the employment rates within 1 year of graduation we found that 84% of those from Hogwarts and only 62% of those from Muggleside were in magical employment. This difference was statistically significant – p-value <0.001. We repeated the analysis out to three years and found that the figures had changed. Now, 89% of Hogwarts graduates and 68% of Muggleside graduates are in magical employment. Again this difference was statistically significant with a p-value of less than 0.01.

Of course, there could be reasons why witches and wizards with different employment potential may have originally been accepted into Hogwarts or not. Such a potential bias in our analysis was examined and carefully excluded. Interestingly, we also examined for any sex difference in employment potential. One of the authors (H. G-W) has long held that witches are superior to wizards and sure enough more females were in magical employment than males irrespective of which school they had attended. In Hogwarts 91% of girls compared with a lamentable 88% of boys managed to get a magical job, while from Muggleside the corresponding numbers were 72% females versus 66% males. In both cases the sex differences were statistically significant ($p<0.05$).

Overall, we may conclude after these extensive investigations that it does matter which form of education a young witch or wizard is exposed to, when we are considering their future employment prospects. Attendance at a traditional magical educational establishment is obviously better than a "muggle-shop". The reasons behind this difference require a detailed exposition and they will be elaborated upon during the presentation.

(553 words!)

Activity 1 Answer & Comments

This conference abstract was requested in an unstructured format, i.e. as a single paragraph without headings. As such it serves as a convenient example to use in this analysis exercise. It should also remind us that even if we are asked for an unstructured abstract, we should always write it as if it were structured – with background, methods, results and conclusion sections.

This abstract is fairly simple to break down, as all good abstracts should be. The title is clear and prominent. Each section begins with a new sentence and, in the case of the final section, with the signpost words "We conclude". Below you will find the abstract sections highlighted to check against your solution.

Title

Predictors of plasma lipoprotein (a) concentration in the West of Scotland Coronary Prevention Study cohort

Background

An elevated plasma lipoprotein (a) [Lp(a)] concentration is an independent risk factor for coronary heart disease. Plasma Lp(a) levels are believed to be predominantly controlled by the *APO(a)* gene, which encodes the apo(a) glycoprotein moiety of the Lp(a) particle. However, other parameters in the lipoprotein profile as well as co-existing disease states or personal traits have been proposed as co-variates.

Methods

In order to examine these potential controlling factors in greater detail than previously possible, 1,760 unrelated Caucasian subjects were studied, from which were identified 907 with a single expressing *APO(a)* allele. This strategy was taken to obviate the difficulty in dealing with the co-expression of different apo(a) isoforms and the resulting compound plasma Lp(a) level. After cube root transformation of the plasma Lp(a) levels to normalise their distribution, a series of correlates were computed.

Results

There was no good correlation between Lp(a) concentration and any other measured lipid or lipoprotein in the lipid profile or with any other variable examined, with the important exception of the length of the expressed apo(a) isoform ($r=-0.491$, $P=0.0001$).

Conclusion

We conclude that in this population the plasma Lp(a) concentration is not predicted by the plasma lipid profile, alcohol intake, or smoking status but is predicted, albeit incompletely, by the length polymorphism of the *APO(a)* gene.

Activity 2 Answer & Comments

Abstract 1

This abstract would undoubtedly score very poorly. First, the title gives little indication of the nature and findings of the study and it is grammatically incorrect. The latter, in itself, might be enough to stop a reviewer in their tracks and prevent them from reading any further. If this did not deter the reviewer the many grammatical and syntactical errors that follow in the body of the abstract would certainly confirm the work's weakness and may consign it to the bin.

The abstract shows many hallmarks of having been written by a non-native English speaker. Abstract writing is difficult at the best of times, but if English is not your first language it is doubly so, and it is imperative that you have it checked by a native speaker. Even with such corrections there are still a number of problems with this work. For example, there is extensive use of abbreviations that are not defined on first usage; there is no background statement to introduce the abstract and its topic; there is the use of a quoted reference to the work of others (Black & Weiss), which has no place in an abstract, and, one of my personal dislikes, the authors have seen fit to use an exclamation mark to emphasise their point. Technical writing of any kind, and especially abstracts should never contain exclamation marks. Your comments and opinions should be stated clearly, not exclaimed.

The length of the abstract is also problematic. The organizers have allowed up to 250 words, but the authors, despite their telegraphic style have only used 206 words to tell their story. This does suggest inattention to the detail of the instructions for submissions or a slapdash approach to the whole writing process.

Overall, it is difficult on a single reading to fathom what the authors have actually done and found. However, a single reading, remember, is all you are likely to be given and it is therefore imperative that your meaning is clearly apparent and easy to see first time round.

It should of course be noted that the authors of this work may be very competent researchers and their work of considerable interest, but all we have to go on to evaluate both these aspects is the 206 words they have submitted. We may know of this group and their excellent reputation may precede them, but remember often your abstract will be reviewed blindly by a conference organizer – i.e. your names and affiliations will be deleted before being passed to a reviewer for their opinion. In this case, your abstract is even more important, for it is literally all they can judge you by.

Abstract 2

This abstract is likely to score highly. The title is clear, contains no cryptic abbreviations and gives the bottom line result of the study. The body of the abstract is presented in a structured format: background, methods, results and conclusion with clear headers for each section. The background consists of three sentences, which are used to define the topic, the problem being addressed and the key abbreviations to be used throughout.

The methods section states clearly what has been done, how it was done and to what. The analytical methods are described very briefly as the authors have made the reasonable assumption that their audience does not need to be told in detail what PCR or in-situ hybridization are. The former stands for polymerase chain reaction, but is such a standard abbreviation, like DNA, that it does not need to be spelled out.

The results are presented succinctly with some specifics (the viral loads in treated and control birds). The results presented are essentially negative – with no significant differences noted. These findings are just as important as positive findings although the latter are routinely given greater priority in journals and conferences. A well-conducted study showing no difference is much more important that any set of equivocal findings or even a strongly positive result that lacks scientific rigour.

The conclusion is a single sentence that echoes the abstract's title and states clearly the main finding of the study.

Overall the authors have presented a very clear, concise and complete description of their study, which only requires a single reading to know what was done, why it was done and what was found. To do so they have used exactly the word limit (250 words) and any conference organizer would welcome such an abstract.

The decision whether this would be accepted for a poster or for an oral presentation would depend on a number of other factors. The abstract obviously demonstrates the competence, both scientific and literary, of the authors but its topic would have to fit with one of the oral sessions that have been planned for the meeting. Also, if there are a large number of similar abstracts all reporting like findings, only one or two may make it to the oral list and the others may be accepted as posters. If, on the other hand, it is just the topic that the organizer needs to complete one of the sessions it will be accepted with alacrity. Writing a good abstract can therefore get you to the conference, but luck as much as anything else, may decide whether you make it to the podium.

Abstract 3

This abstract would likely score somewhere between that of Abstract 1 and Abstract 2. Overall, it is more clearly written than Abstract 1, but lacks the crystal clarity of Abstract 2.

The title, although clearly setting out what was done and where, does not include any indication of the findings. Perhaps a more informative title would have been:

Multi-drug resistant psittacosis infection control assessment in veterinary practices in rural Madagascar indicates need for improvement.

The body of the abstract is structured like that in Abstract 2, which is to its credit. However, the results section is split into two paragraphs, which is unnecessary. Key abbreviations are defined on first use and there is a relatively clear line of argument from a statement of the problem, the methods used and the results obtained. However, there are a few grey areas. For example, although a number of results are given as percentages, nowhere in the abstract is it specified how many veterinary staff were assessed. Similarly, the use of the term *compliance* as an absolute rather than relative term implies that more than a certain level of face-mask use constituted compliance and less than that level a lack of compliance. The authors have, however, not included this cut-off. Not infrequently crucial pieces of information like this are missing from an abstract. In such cases, the authors have not consciously decided to leave it out; it is more likely that they were simply so close to the data and so familiar with their study that they forgot they had to mention it.

Activity 3 Answer & Comments

Prof. Granger-Weasley's first draft has a lot of problems that we can fix quickly and a few that will take a little more thought.

We need a title, but this should be the last component we compose. The draft is almost three times as long as it should be, so we will need to make some significant cuts. There is excessive detail in parts and an overlong background section that is largely repetitive. There are also a number of stylistic problems including the use of contractions like "we've", the introduction of personal comments like "One of the authors (H. G-W) has long held that witches are superior to wizards..." and "obviously" and Prof. Granger-Weasley has committed the sin of using an exclamation mark in technical writing.

Taking all these points into consideration I have proposed the following revision for Prof. Granger-Weasley. This, of course, is not the only solution, but one with which you can compare your own version.

Title: Charm schools? Magical unemployment is higher in graduates of non-traditional schools of magic.

Authors: Granger-Weasley, H.J., Potter, H.J. and Potter, G.M.

Magical unemployment has increased from 10-35% in the last decade. The reasons are unclear, but an increase in non-traditional schooling within the magical community may have contributed. We examined the employment records of those graduating between 2001-2006 from a traditional school of magic [Hogwarts School of Witchcraft and Wizardry (HSWW)] and compared them with those from a non-traditional school [Muggleside Secondary Modern (MSM)]. 256 graduates of HSWW and 287 graduates of MSM were assessed using an owl delivered questionnaire parchment with a closed question design. The response rates were 93% (HSWW) and 87% (MSM). Within 12 months of graduation 84% of HSWW graduates were in magical employment compared with 62% of MSM graduates ($p<0.001$). Within 36 months of graduation the corresponding figures were 89% and 68% ($p<0.01$). These significant differences remained even after adjustment for potential confounders relating to entrance selection bias. A small, but significant, difference between the sexes was also observed irrespective of education, with more witches securing magical employment than wizards (HSWW: 91% vs 88%, $p<0.05$; MSM: 72% vs 66%, $p<0.05$). Thus, graduation from a traditional school confers an employment advantage over that from a non-traditional or muggle school. Possible reasons for this advantage will be discussed.

(200 words)

SUGGESTIONS FOR FURTHER STUDY

I believe the only way to learn how to write is to write, rewrite and then have you work critiqued by others. When it comes to technical writing such as Abstract writing you also have to read as much as possible – study the abstract book from last year's conference and look at the abstracts of the original articles in the highest impact journals in your field.

This Quick Guide has set out the key approach you should take when it comes to putting pen to paper, but you may feel you need more help either with the mechanics of your writing like grammar and style or with your overall approach to technical writing. As always there are more books written on this subject than you could ever hope to read, so I have listed several below that you may find useful.

All these books can be found individually on Amazon or you will find them listed together for convenience on my website www.academic-skills.com

Academic Writing Guides

Writing for Academic Journals. Rowena Murray. Open University Press, 2nd edition. ISBN: 978-0335234585.

Also available for kindle download.

> Rowena Murray is a respected teacher who has written a number of excellent books on the practicalities of academic writing in its various forms. This book unravels the process of writing academic papers. It tells readers what good papers look like and how they can be written.

How to Write a Paper. George M. Hall (Ed). Wiley-Blackwell, 4th edition, 2008. ISBN: 978-1405167734.

Also available for kindle download.

> This is a useful multi-author book from the celebrated BMJ series that defines the publication process for academic papers. The book includes chapters entitled: "Titles, abstracts and authors" and "How to prepare an abstract for a scientific meeting".

Brilliant Writing Tips for Students (Pocket Study Skills). Julia Copus. Palgrave Macmillan, 2009. ISBN: 978-0230220027.

> This short book contains a wealth of useful tips on punctuation, style, grammar and essay structure, as well as numerous examples and self-help exercises.

General Writing Guides

The Elements of Style. William Strunk Jr. Filiquarian Publishing, 2007. ISBN: 978-1599869339.

> The classic (American) English style guide, which was originally written in 1918, is both succinct and accessible. It concentrates on "a few essentials, the rules of usage and principles of composition most commonly violated."

Pocket Fowler's Modern English Usage. Robert Allen (Ed). OUP Oxford, 2nd edition, 2008. ISBN: 978-0199232581.

> Although it could hardly be described as a pocket book this edition of the classic Fowler's Modern English Usage is invaluable and will provide the user with what many regard as the definitive answers to any question relating to written English.

The Penguin Writer's Manual. Martin Manser & Stephen Curtis. Penguin, 2004. ISBN: 978-0140514896.

Also available for kindle download.

> This is a general writing guide that would be a useful addition to any reference bookshelf. Is it 'assume' or 'presume'; 'till' or 'until'; 'that' or 'which'? You will find all the answers here.

Non-native English Writing Guides

Academic Writing: A Handbook for International Students (Routledge Study Guides) Stephen Bailey. Routledge, 2nd edition, 2006. ISBN: 978-0415384209.

Also available for kindle download.

> This book would be useful for non-native English speakers who need to write technical, academic English. The book presents a practical writing course with exercises that will enable the

international student to meet the required standards of writing and use an appropriate style for essays, exams and dissertations.

Presentation Skill Guides

Our Speaker Today – A Guide to Effective Lecturing. Allan Gaw. SA Press, 2010. ISBN: 978-0956324214.

Also available for kindle download.

> Because I couldn't find a book that I thought included all the different aspects of presentation design, dealing with questions, and slide preparation with a strongly practical slant I felt the need to write one – forgive me the indulgence of recommending my own book, but I do feel it's the one that fits the bill if you need help in preparing that first conference presentation.

Poster Making Guides

Scientist's Guide to Poster Presentations. Peter J. Gosling. Springer 1999. ISBN 978-0306460760.

Also available for kindle download.

> This book provides a very practical and comprehensive approach to poster design, manufacture, transport and presentation with lots of examples.

INDEX